UKULELE

CHRISTMAS SONGS WITH THREE CHORDS

ISBN 978-1-5400-9762-0

HAL•LEONARD®

Visit Hal Leonard Online at
www.halleonard.com

Contact Us:
Hal Leonard
7777 West Bluemound Road
Milwaukee, WI 53213
Email: info@halleonard.com

In Europe, contact:
Hal Leonard Europe Limited
42 Wigmore Street
Marylebone, London, W1U 2RN
Email: info@halleonardeurope.com

In Australia, contact:
Hal Leonard Australia Pty. Ltd.
4 Lentara Court
Cheltenham, Victoria, 3192 Australia
Email: info@halleonard.com.au

CONTENTS

Almost Day

Words and Music by Huddie Ledbetter

First note

Verse
Square Dance tempo

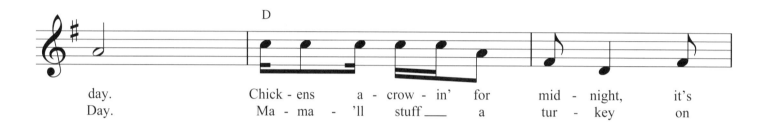

1. Chick - ens a - crow - in' for mid - night, it's al - most
2. Ma - ma - 'll stuff ___ a tur - key on Christ - mas

day. Chick - ens a - crow - in' for mid - night, it's
Day. Ma - ma - 'll stuff ___ a tur - key on

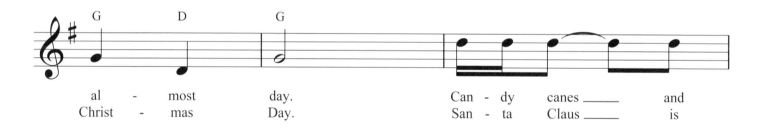

al - most day. Can - dy canes ___ and
Christ - mas Day. San - ta Claus ___ is

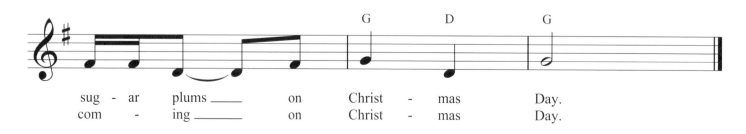

sug - ar plums ___ on Christ - mas Day. Can - dy canes ___ and
com - ing ___ on Christ - mas Day. San - ta Claus ___ is

sug - ar plums ___ on Christ - mas Day.
com - ing ___ on Christ - mas Day.

The Chipmunk Song

Words and Music by Ross Bagdasarian

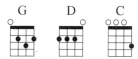

First note

Verse
Happily

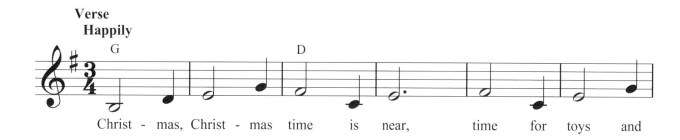

Christ - mas, Christ - mas time is near, time for toys and

time for cheer. We've been good, but we can't last.

Hur - ry, Christ - mas, hur - ry fast! Want a plane that

loops the loop. Me, I want a Hu - la - hoop. We can

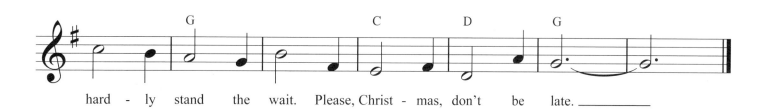

hard - ly stand the wait. Please, Christ - mas, don't be late. _____

Christmas Is A-Comin'
(May God Bless You)

Words and Music by Frank Luther

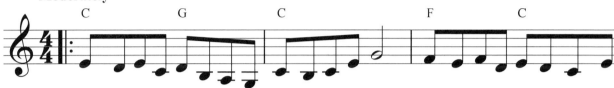

First note

Verse
Moderately

1. Christ-mas is a-com-in' and the geese are get-tin' fat. Please to put a pen-ny in a
2. Christ-mas is a-com-in' and the lights are on the tree. How a-bout a tur-key leg for
3. Christ-mas is a-com-in' and the egg is in the nog. Please to let me sit a-round your

poor man's hat. If you have - n't got a pen-ny, then a ha' pen-ny - 'll do. If you
poor old me? If you have - n't got a tur-key leg, a tur - key wing-'ll do. If you
old yule log. If you'd rath-er I did - n't sit a-round, to stand a-round-'ll do. If you'd

Chorus

have - n't got a ha' pen - ny, may God bless you. God bless you, gen-tle-men,
have - n't got a tur - key wing, may God bless you. God bless you, gen-tle-men,
rath-er I did - n't stand a - round, may God bless you. God bless you, gen-tle-men,

1., 2.

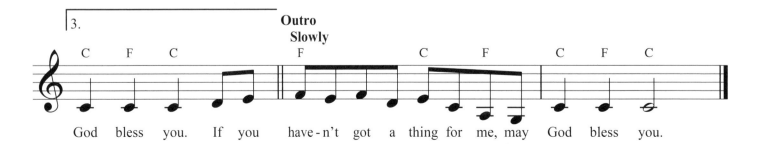

God bless you. If you have - n't got a ha' pen - ny, may God bless you.
God bless you. If you have - n't got a tur - key wing, may God bless you.
God bless you. If you'd rath-er I did - n't stand a - round, may

3.

Outro
Slowly

God bless you. If you have - n't got a thing for me, may God bless you.

Grandma Got Run Over by a Reindeer

Words and Music by Randy Brooks

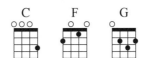

First note

Chorus
Moderately bright

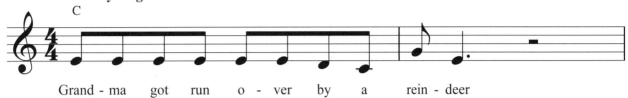

Grand - ma got run o - ver by a rein - deer

walk-ing home from our house Christ-mas Eve. You can say there's no such thing as

San - ta, but as for me and Grand-pa, we be - lieve.

Chorus

Grand-ma got run o - ver by a rein-deer walk-ing home from our house Christ-mas

Eve. You can say there's no such thing as San - ta, but

as for me and Grand-pa, we be - lieve.

Frosty the Snow Man

Words and Music by Steve Nelson and Jack Rollins

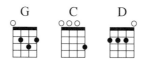

First note

Verse
Moderately fast

1. Frost - y, the snow man was a jol - ly hap - py soul, with a
2. Frost - y, the snow man knew the sun was hot that day, so he

corn - cob pipe and a but - ton nose and two eyes made out of coal.
said, "Let's run and we'll have some fun now be - fore I melt a - way."

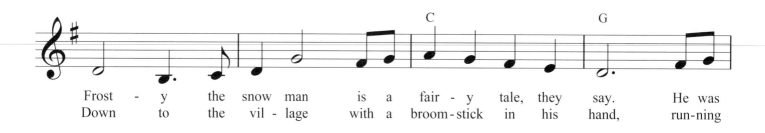

Frost - y the snow man is a fair - y tale, they say. He was
Down to the vil - lage with a broom - stick in his hand, He run - ning

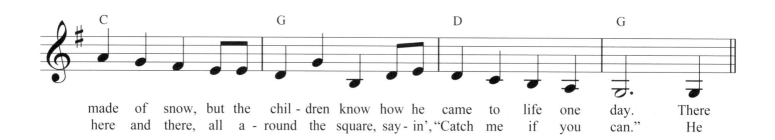

made of snow, but the chil - dren know how he came to life one day. There
here and there, all a - round the square, say - in', "Catch me if you can." He

Bridge

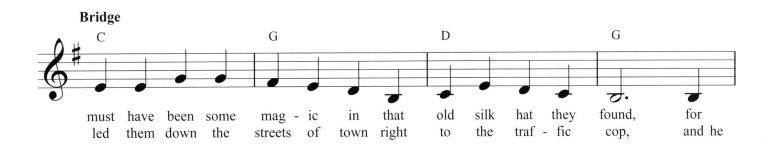

must have been some mag - ic in that old silk hat they found, for
led them down the streets of town right to the traf - fic cop, and he

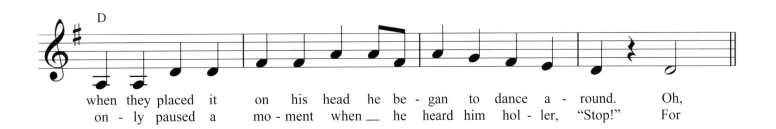

when they placed it on his head he be - gan to dance a - round. Oh,
on - ly paused a mo - ment when — he heard him hol - ler, "Stop!" For

Outro-Verse

Frost - y the snow man was a - live as he could be, and the
Frost - y the snow man had to hur - ry on his way, but he

chil - dren say he could laugh and play just the same as you and me.
waved good - bye say - in', "Don't you cry, I'll be back a - gain some - day,"

Outro

Thump-et - y thump thump, thump-et - y thump thump, look at Frost - y go.

Thump-et - y thump thump, thump-et - y thump thump, o - ver the hills of snow.

Grandma's Killer Fruitcake

Words and Music by Elmo Shropshire and Rita Abrams

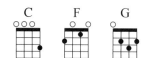

First note

Verse
Country Polka, in 2

1. The hol - i - days were up - on us and things were go - in'
2., 3. *See additional lyrics*

fine, till the day I heard the door - bell and a chill ran up my

spine. I grabbed the wife and chil - dren as the post - man wheeled it

in. A year - ly Christ - mas night - mare has just come back a -

Chorus

gain. It was hard - er than the head of Un - cle Buck - y,

heav - y as a ser - mon of Preach - er Luck - y. One's e - nough to give the whole

state of Ken - tuck - y a great big bel - ly - ache. It was

dens - er than a drove of barn - yard tur - keys, tough - er than a truck - load of

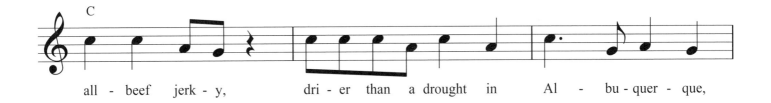

all - beef jerk - y, dri - er than a drought in Al - bu - quer - que,

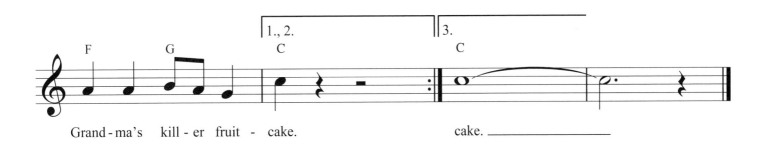

Grand - ma's kill - er fruit - cake. cake.

Additional Lyrics

2. Now, I've had to swallow some marginal fare at our family feast.
   I even downed Aunt Dolly's possom pie just to keep the family peace.
   I winced at Wilma's gizzard mousse, but said it tasted fine.
   But that lethal weapon that Grandma bakes is where I draw the line.

3. It's early Christmas morning, the phone rings us awake.
   It's Grandma, Pa, she wants to know how'd we like the cake.
   "Well, Grandma, I never. Uh, we couldn't. It was, uh, unbelievable, that's for sure!
   What's that you say? Oh, no, Grandma. Puh-leez don't send us any more!"

Here Comes Santa Claus
(Right Down Santa Claus Lane)

Words and Music by Gene Autry and Oakley Haldeman

First note

Verse
Moderately, in 2

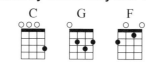

1. Here comes San - ta Claus! Here comes San - ta Claus! Right down San - ta Claus
2.–4. *See additional lyrics*

Lane! Vix - en and Blitz - en and all his rein-deer are pull - ing on the rein.

Bells are ring - ing, chil-dren sing - ing, all is mer-ry and bright. Hang your stock-ings and

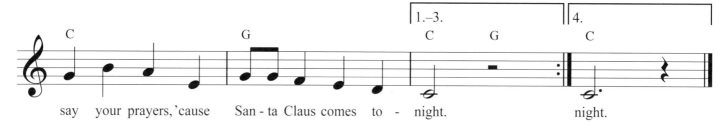

say your prayers, 'cause San - ta Claus comes to - night. night.

Additional Lyrics

2. Here comes Santa Claus! Here comes Santa Claus!
Right down Santa Claus Lane!
He's got a bag that is filled with toys
For the boys and girls again.
Hear those sleigh bells jingle, jangle,
What a beautiful sight.
Jump in bed, cover up your head,
'Cause Santa Claus comes tonight.

3. Here comes Santa Claus! Here comes Santa Claus!
Right down Santa Claus Lane!
He doesn't care if you're rich or poor,
For he loves you just the same.
Santa knows that we're God's children;
That makes ev'rything right.
Fill your hearts with a Christmas cheer,
'Cause Santa Claus comes tonight.

4. Here comes Santa Claus! Here comes Santa Claus!
Right down Santa Claus Lane!
He'll come around when the chimes ring out;
Then it's Christmas morn again.
Peace on earth will come to all
If we just follow the light.
Let's give thanks to the Lord above,
'Cause Santa Claus comes tonight.

Mary's Little Boy

Words and Music by Massie Patterson and Sammy Heyward

Additional Lyrics

2. Soldiers looked for the little boy,
Soldiers looked for the little boy,
Soldiers looked for the little boy,
And they said His name was Wonderful.

3. Wise men came running from the East,
Wise men came running from the East,
Wise men came running from the East,
And they said His name was Wonderful.

I'll Be Home on Christmas Day

Words and Music by Michael Jarrett

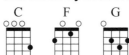

First note

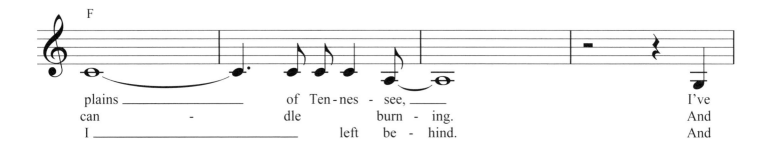

1. From the hills of Geor - gia, a-cross the
2. It's been so man - y _____ times be-fore she left that
3. There were times I'd think a - bout _____ her, all the love

plains _____ of Ten - nes - see, _____ I've
can - dle burn - ing. And
I _____ left be - hind. And

seen and I've done _____ most ev - 'ry-thing that a
all too _____ man - y tears that fell, my
mem - o - ries _____ still lin - ger with -

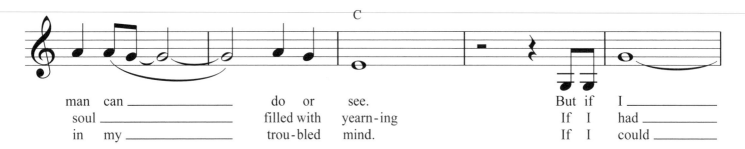

man can _____ do or see. But if I _____
soul _____ filled with yearn - ing If I had _____
in my _____ trou - bled mind. If I could _____

_____ could on - ly bor - row one dream _____ from yes - ter-
_____ an - y sense at all, I'd just be _____ on my
_____ set a - side my pride, then I'd be _____ on my

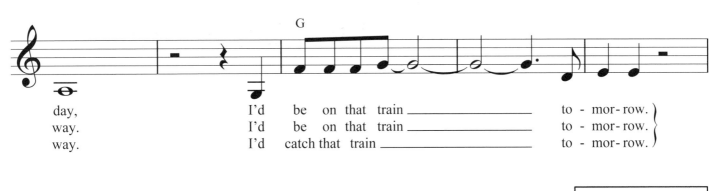

day,
way.
way.

I'd be on that train _____ to - mor - row.
I'd be on that train _____ to - mor - row.
I'd catch that train _____ to - mor - row.

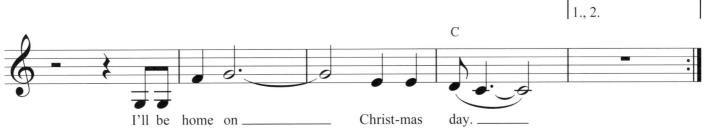

1., 2.

I'll be home on _____ Christ-mas day. _____

3.

Outro

If I had _____ an - y sense at all, _____ I'd just

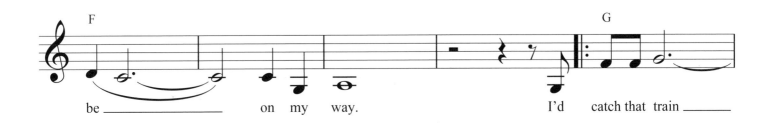

be _____ on my way. I'd catch that train _____

1.

_____ to - mor - row. I'll be home on _____ Christ-mas

2.

day. _____ I said, I'll home on _____ Christ-mas day. _____

It Won't Seem Like Christmas
(Without You)

Words and Music by J.A. Balthrop

First note

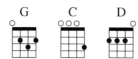

Chorus

Moderately

Oh, it won't seem like Christ-mas, oh, with-out you,

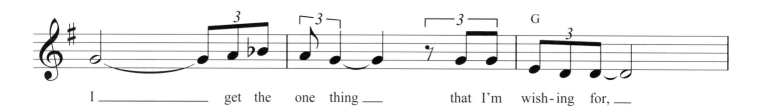

for too man-y miles ___ are be-tween. But if

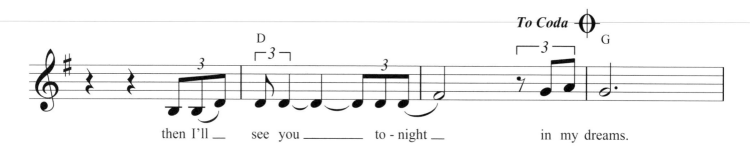

I ___ get the one thing ___ that I'm wish-ing for, ___

To Coda

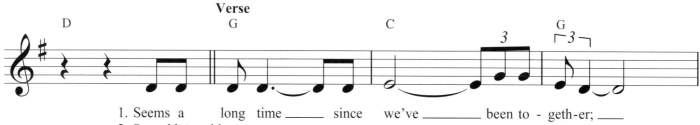

then I'll ___ see you ___ to-night ___ in my dreams.

Verse

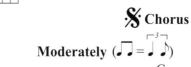

1. Seems a long time ___ since we've ___ been to-geth-er; ___
2. *See additional lyrics*

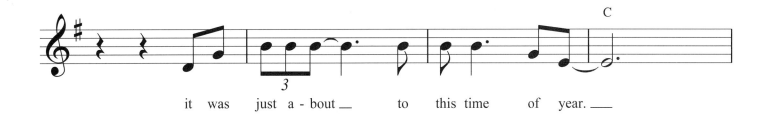

it was just a-bout ___ to this time of year. ___

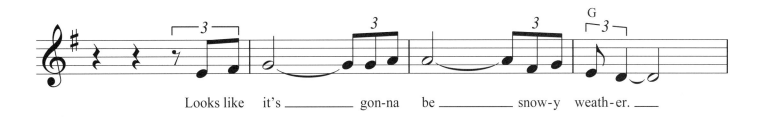

Looks like it's ___ gon-na be ___ snow-y weath-er. ___

How I wish that you could be here. ___

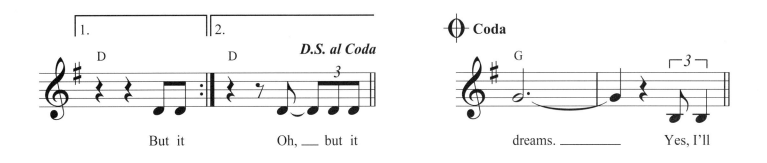

But it | Oh, ___ but it | dreams. ___ | Yes, I'll

see you to-night in my dreams. ___

Additional Lyrics

2. In the distance I hear sleigh bells ringing.
   The holly's so pretty this year;
   And the carol that somebody's singing
   Reminds me of our Christmas last year.

The Little Drummer Boy

Words and Music by Harry Simeone, Henry Onorati and Katherine Davis

First note

Verse
Moderately slow, in 2

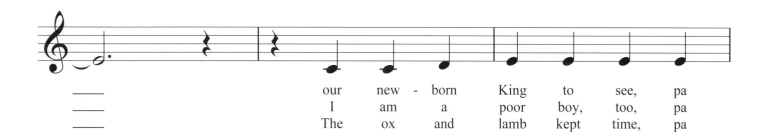

1. Come, they told me, pa rum pum pum pum, ___
2. Ba - by told Je - su, pa rum pum pum pum, ___
3. Mar - y nod - ded, pa rum pum pum pum. ___

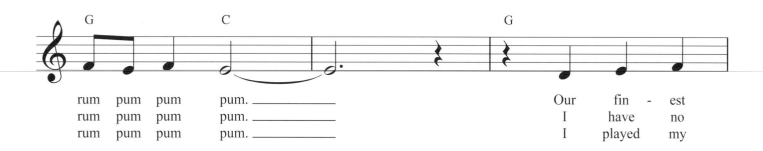

___ our new - born King to see, pa
___ I am a poor boy, too, pa
___ The ox and lamb kept time, pa

rum pum pum pum. ___ Our fin - est
rum pum pum pum. ___ I have no
rum pum pum pum. ___ I played my

gifts we bring, pa rum pum pum pum, ___
gift to bring, pa rum pum pum pum, ___
drum for Him, pa rum pum pum pum. ___

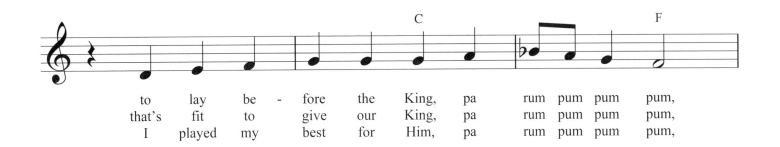

to	lay	be	-	fore	the	King,	pa	rum	pum	pum	pum,
that's	fit	to		give	our	King,	pa	rum	pum	pum	pum,
I	played	my		best	for	Him,	pa	rum	pum	pum	pum,

rum	pum	pum	pum,	rum	pum	pum	pum, _____
rum	pum	pum	pum,	rum	pum	pum	pum. _____
rum	pum	pum	pum,	rum	pum	pum	pum. _____

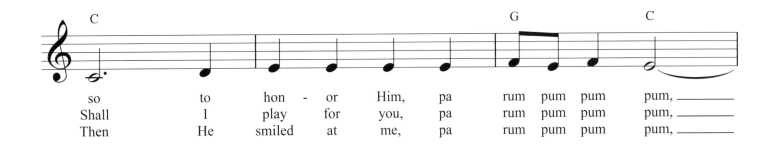

so		to	hon	-	or	Him,	pa	rum	pum	pum	pum, _____
Shall		I	play		for	you,	pa	rum	pum	pum	pum, _____
Then		He	smiled		at	me,	pa	rum	pum	pum	pum, _____

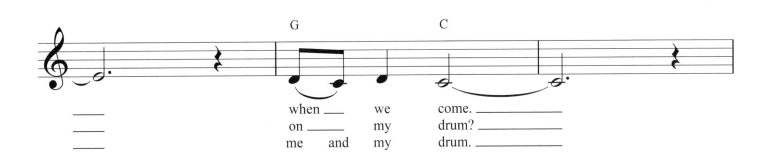

_____					
_____	when	__	we	come. _____
_____	on	_____	my	drum? _____
	me	and	my	drum. _____

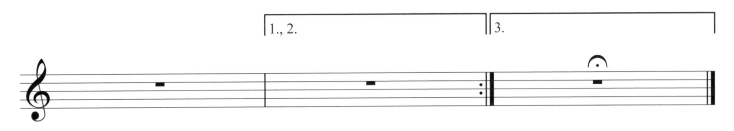

1., 2.   3.

Merry Christmas, Baby

Words and Music by Lou Baxter and Johnny Moore

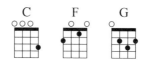

First note

Verse
Moderate Blues

1. Mer-ry Christ-mas, ba - by; you sure ___ did treat me nice. ___

___ Mer - ry Christ-mas, ba - by; you sure ___ did treat me

nice. ___ Gave me a dia - mond ring for Christ-mas;

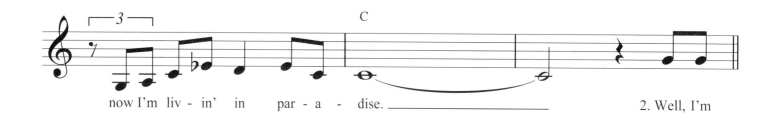

now I'm liv - in' in par - a - dise. ___ 2. Well, I'm

Verse

feel - in' might-y fine, ___ got good mu - sic on my ra - di - o. ___

Well, I'm feel-in' might-y fine, ___ got good mu-sic on my ra-di-o. ___

Well, I want to kiss you, ba - by,

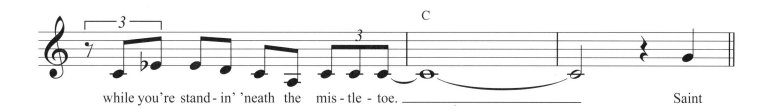

while you're stand-in' 'neath the mis-tle-toe. ___ Saint

Outro-Verse

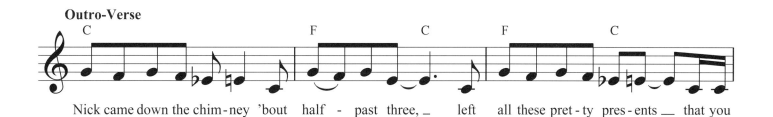

Nick came down the chim-ney 'bout half-past three, ___ left all these pret-ty pres-ents ___ that you

see be-fore me. ___ Mer-ry Christ-mas, lit-tle ba - by; you sure ___ been good to

me. ___ I have-n't had a drink this morn-in', ___ but I'm

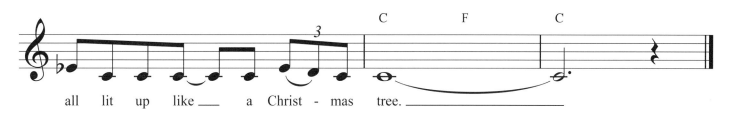

all lit up like ___ a Christ-mas tree. ___

A Merry, Merry Christmas to You

Music and Lyrics by Johnny Marks

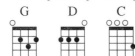

First note

Chorus
Spirited, in 1

Mer - ry, mer - ry, mer - ry, mer - ry, mer - ry

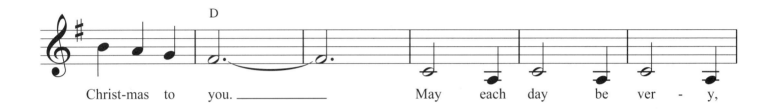

Christ-mas to you. _____ May each day be ver - y,

ver - y hap - py all the year through. _____ A-

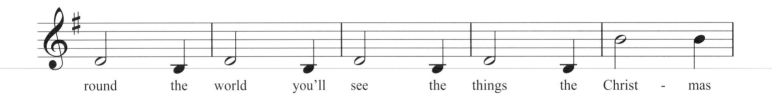

round the world you'll see the things the Christ - mas

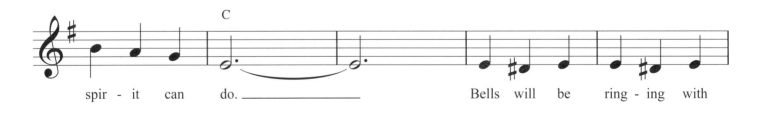

spir - it can do. _____ Bells will be ring - ing with

ev - 'ry - one sing - ing, "A mer - ry Christ-mas to you!" _____

Pretty Paper

Words and Music by Willie Nelson

First note

Chorus
Slowly, with expression

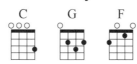

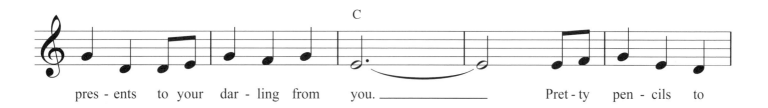

Pret-ty pa - per, pret-ty rib - bons of blue. _____ Wrap your

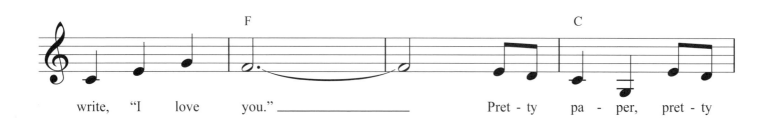

pres - ents to your dar - ling from you. _____ Pret-ty pen - cils to

write, "I love you." _____ Pret-ty pa - per, pret-ty

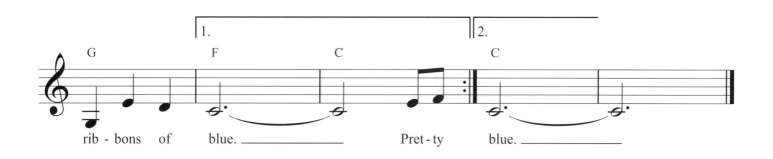

1.
rib - bons of blue. _____ Pret-ty

2.
blue. _____

Shake Me I Rattle
(Squeeze Me I Cry)

Words and Music by Hal Hackady and Charles Naylor

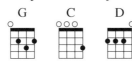

First note

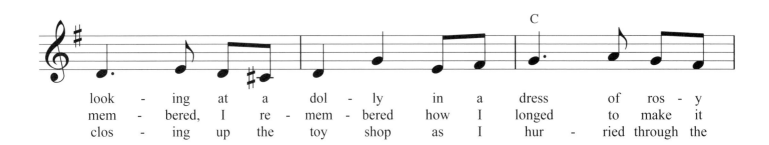

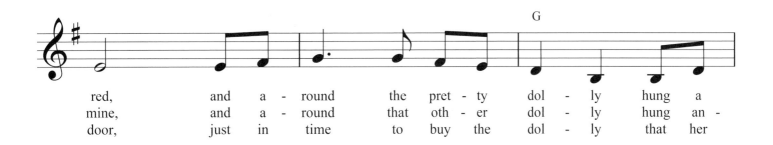

red, and a - round the pret - ty dol - ly hung a
mine, and a - round that oth - er dol - ly hung an -
door, just in time to buy the dol - ly that her

Chorus

lit - tle sign that said: Shake me, I rat - tle.
oth - er lit - tle sign: Shake me, I rat - tle.
heart was long - ing for. Shake me, I rat - tle.

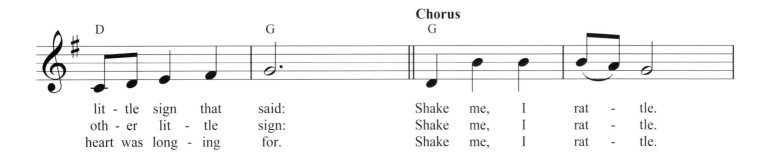

Squeeze me, I cry. As I stood there be -
Squeeze me, I cry. I had count - ed my
Squeeze me, I cry. And I gave her the

side her, I could hear her sigh. } Shake me, I
pen - nies, just a pen - ny shy. }
dol - ly that we both had longed to buy. }

rat - tle. Squeeze me, I cry. Please take me

1., 2. | 3.

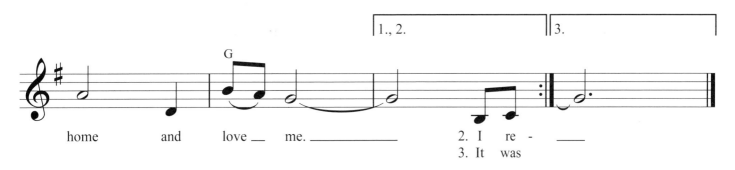

home and love _ me. _____ 2. I re - _
                                3. It was

25

Silver Bells

from the Paramount Picture THE LEMON DROP KID

Words and Music by Jay Livingston and Ray Evans

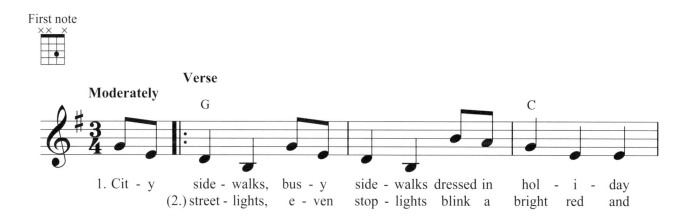

First note
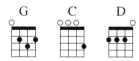

Verse

Moderately

1. Cit - y side - walks, bus - y side - walks dressed in hol - i - day
(2.) street - lights, e - ven stop - lights blink a bright red and

style, in the air there's a feel - ing of Christ - mas.
green, as the shop - pers rush home with their treas - ures.

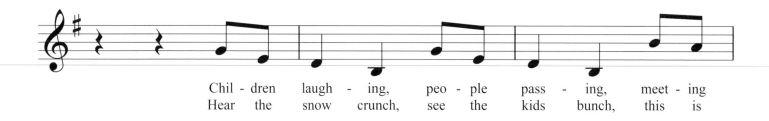

Chil - dren laugh - ing, peo - ple pass - ing, meet - ing
Hear the snow crunch, see the kids bunch, this is

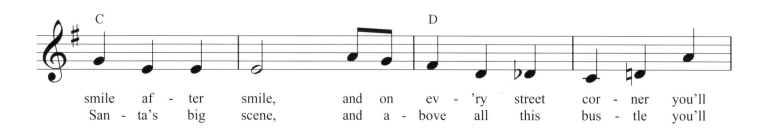

smile af - ter smile, and on ev - 'ry street cor - ner you'll
San - ta's big scene, and a - bove all this bus - tle you'll

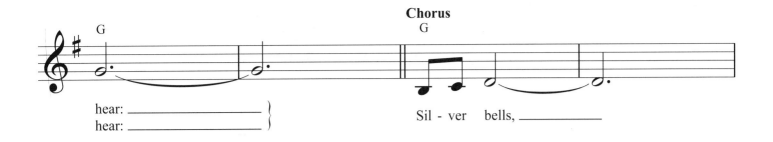

Chorus

hear: _____
hear: _____

Sil - ver bells, _____

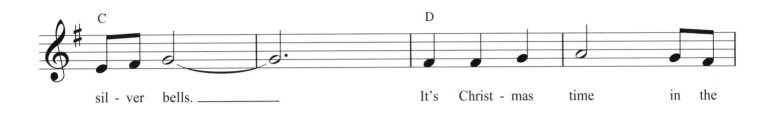

sil - ver bells. _____ It's Christ - mas time in the

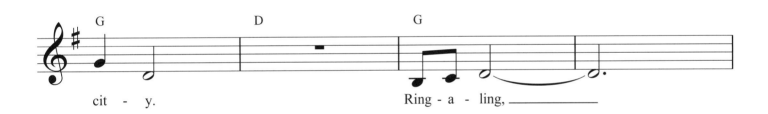

cit - y. Ring - a - ling, _____

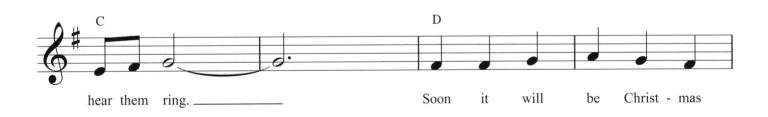

hear them ring. _____ Soon it will be Christ - mas

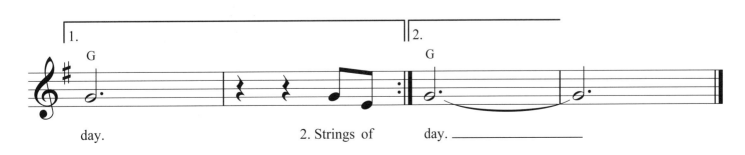

1.

day.

2. Strings of

2.

day. _____

What a Merry Christmas This Could Be

Words and Music by Hank Cochran and Harlan Howard

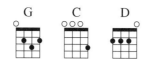

First note

What a mer - ry Christ - mas this could be

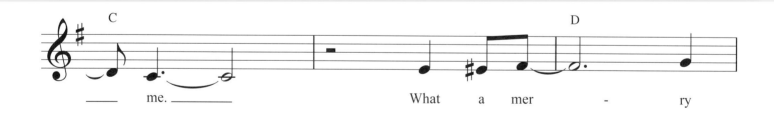

if you _____ would just come back _____ to _____

_____ me _____ and say that you'd for - giv - en _____

_____ me. _____ What a mer - ry

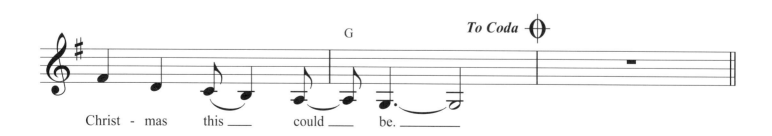

Christ - mas this _____ could _____ be. _____

Verse

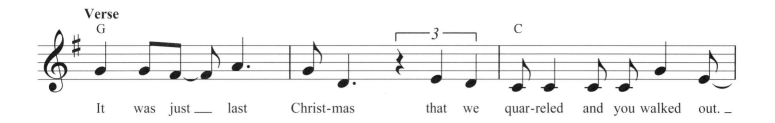

It was just _ last Christ-mas that we quar-reled and you walked out. _

_ I knew _ I was wrong, _ but you'd _ come

back; I _ had no doubt. Now a year _ has

rolled a - round; _ it's Christ-mas once a - gain, and

what I'd give if you'd _ come _ walk - in' _ in.

D.S. al Coda   **Coda**   **Outro**

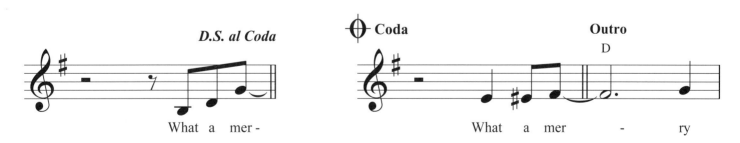

What a mer -   What a mer - ry

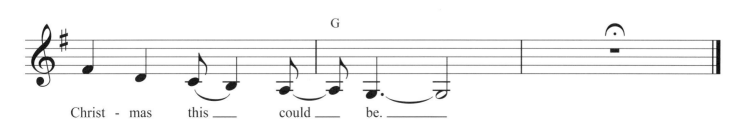

Christ - mas this _ could _ be. _

Where Are You Christmas?

from DR. SEUSS' HOW THE GRINCH STOLE CHRISTMAS

Words and Music by Will Jennings, James Horner and Mariah Carey

First note

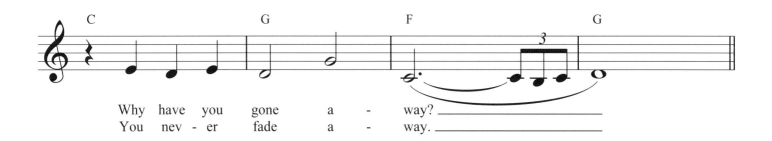

Verse
Gently, in 2

1. Where are you, Christ - mas? Why can't I find you?
4. I feel you, Christ - mas. I know I found you.

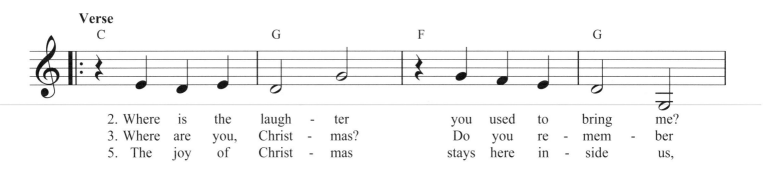

Why have you gone a - way? _____
You nev - er fade a - way. _____

Verse

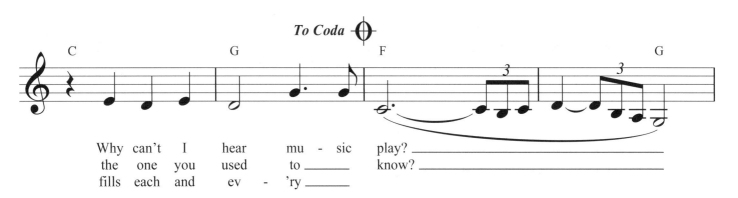

2. Where is the laugh - ter you used to bring me?
3. Where are you, Christ - mas? Do you re - mem - ber
5. The joy of Christ - mas stays here in - side us,

To Coda

Why can't I hear mu - sic play? _____
the one you used to _____ know? _____
fills each and ev - 'ry _____

My world is chang - ing. __ I'm re - ar - rang - ing.
I'm not the same one. __ See what the time's done.

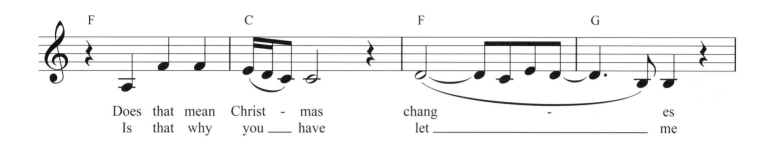

Does that mean Christ - mas chang - es
Is that why you __ have let __ me

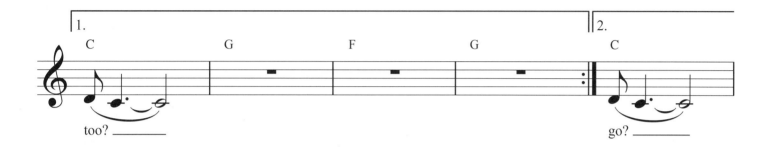

1.
too? __

2.
go? __

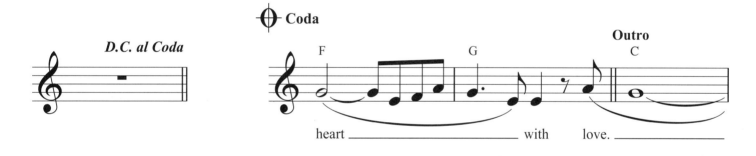

D.C. al Coda

Coda

Outro

heart __ with love. __

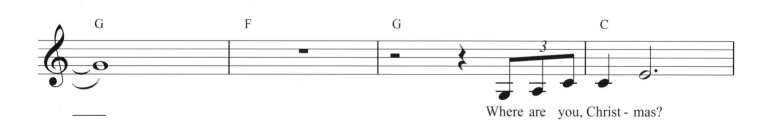

__

Where are you, Christ - mas?

Fill your heart with love.

The Best Collections for Ukulele

The Best Songs Ever

70 songs have now been arranged for ukulele. Includes: Always • Bohemian Rhapsody • Memory • My Favorite Things • Over the Rainbow • Piano Man • What a Wonderful World • Yesterday • You Raise Me Up • and more.

00282413 . . . . $17.99

Disney Hits for Ukulele

Play 23 of your favorite Disney songs on your ukulele. Includes: The Bare Necessities • Cruella De Vil • Do You Want to Build a Snowman? • Kiss the Girl • Lava • Let It Go • Once upon a Dream • A Whole New World • and more.

00151250 . . . . $14.99

Top Hits of 2019

Strum your favorite songs of 2019 on the uke. Includes: Bad Guy (Billie Eilish) • I Don't Care (Ed Sheeran & Justin Bieber) • ME! (Taylor Swift) • Old Town Road (Remix) (Lil Nas X feat. Billy Ray Cyrus) • Senorita (Shawn Mendes & Camila Cabello) • Someone You Loved (Lewis Capaldi) • and more.

00302274 . . . . $14.99

Campfire Songs for Ukulele

30 favorites to sing as you roast marshmallows and strum your uke around the campfire. Includes: God Bless the U.S.A. • Hallelujah • The House of the Rising Sun • I Walk the Line • Puff the Magic Dragon • Wagon Wheel • You Are My Sunshine • and more.

00129170 . . . . $14.99

First 50 Songs You Should Play on Ukulele

An amazing collection of 50 accessible, must-know favorites: Edelweiss • Hey, Soul Sister • I Walk the Line • I'm Yours • Imagine • Over the Rainbow • Peaceful Easy Feeling • The Rainbow Connection • Riptide • and many more.

00149250 . . . . $14.99

The Ukulele 3 Chord Songbook

If you know three chords, you can play these 50 great hits! Songs include: Bad Moon Rising • A Boy Named Sue • King of the Road • Leaving on a Jet Plane • Shelter from the Storm • Time for Me to Fly • Twist and Shout • and many more.

00141143 . . . . $16.99

The Daily Ukulele

compiled and arranged by Liz and Jim Beloff
Strum a different song everyday with easy arrangements of 365 of your favorite songs in one big songbook! Includes favorites by the Beatles, Beach Boys, and Bob Dylan, folk songs, pop songs, kids' songs, Christmas carols, and Broadway and Hollywood tunes, all with a spiral binding for ease of use.

00240356 . . . . $39.99

The Ukulele 4 Chord Songbook

With just 4 chords, you can play 50 hot songs on your ukulele! Songs include: Brown Eyed Girl • Do Wah Diddy Diddy • Hey Ya! • Ho Hey • Jessie's Girl • Let It Be • One Love • Stand by Me • Toes • With or Without You • and many more.

00142050 . . . . $16.99

The Ultimate Ukulele Fake Book

Uke enthusiasts will love this giant, spiral-bound collection of over 400 songs for uke! Includes: Crazy • Dancing Queen • Downtown • Fields of Gold • Happy • Hey Jude • 7 Years • Summertime • Thinking Out Loud • Thriller • Wagon Wheel • and more.

00175500 . . . . $45.00

The Daily Ukulele – Leap Year Edition

366 More Songs for Better Living
compiled and arranged by Liz and Jim Beloff
An amazing second volume with 366 MORE songs for you to master each day of a leap year! Includes: Ain't No Sunshine • Calendar Girl • I Got You Babe • Lean on Me • Moondance • and many, many more.

00240681 . . . . $39.99

Simple Songs for Ukulele

50 favorites for standard G-C-E-A ukulele tuning, including: All Along the Watchtower • Can't Help Falling in Love • Don't Worry, Be Happy • Ho Hey • I'm Yours • King of the Road • Sweet Home Alabama • You Are My Sunshine • and more.

00156815 . . . . $14.99

Ukulele – The Most Requested Songs

Strum & Sing Series
Cherry Lane Music
Nearly 50 favorites all expertly arranged for ukulele! Includes: Bubbly • Build Me Up Buttercup • Cecilia • Georgia on My Mind • Kokomo • L-O-V-E • Your Body Is a Wonderland • and dozens more.

02501453 . . . . $14.99